HAROLD KLEMP

THE
LOVING
HEART

HAROLD KLEMP

ECKANKAR
Minneapolis
www.Eckankar.org

ABOUT THIS BOOK: *The Loving Heart* is compiled from Harold Klemp's writings. These selections originally appeared in his books published by Eckankar.

The Loving Heart

Printed in USA
Compiled by John Kulick
Edited by Patrick Carroll, Joan Klemp, and Anthony Moore
Cover photo: Rolf Nussbaumer/Minden Pictures
Author photo by Robert Huntley
Cover design by Doug Munson

Library of Congress Cataloging-in-Publication Data
Klemp, Harold.
    [Selections. 2011]
    The loving heart / Harold Klemp.
        p. cm.
    ISBN 978-1-57043-332-0 (hardcover : alk. paper)
    1. Spiritual life—Eckankar (Organization) 2. Eckankar (Organization)—Doctrines. I. Title
    BP605.E3K5654 2010
    299'.93—dc22
                                                2010011852

♾ This paper meets the requirements of ANSI/NISO Z39.48-1992 (Permanence of Paper).

Contents

DEAR READER

How can you become the loving heart? The secret is held within the pages of this simple and beautiful seventh volume in Harold Klemp's award-winning Immortality of Soul series.

In *The Loving Heart*, Harold Klemp shows how love is the one constant, the beginning and the end of every experience we have in our lives. By reflecting on the powerful contemplation seeds in this book, you can greatly enhance your ability to give and receive love every day.

As you make your way, step-by-step, to spiritual freedom, you learn the secret of serving all life. You learn to accept God's pure love in your life and become its carrier—the loving heart.

BE A MODEL OF LOVE

The highest love is a pure love for God.

A pure love for another is the same as a pure love for God. There is no difference.

Those with pure love do all they can
to let their loved ones grow in every way.

*L*ove others more. Then, loving yourself just happens.

*R*eal love is selfless. We do continual acts of kindness to make the way easier for our loved ones.

*S*pirituallly healthy people like to be
a ray of sunshine for the ones they love.

*N*ot *to get attached* is often taken to mean "not to get involved." It actually means not to let your idea of how things should be dictate the relationship. That kind of love has strings attached.

*T*he real meaning of detached love is to let others exist without forcing our will upon them. That is spiritual love.

*N*o matter how great your love for each other, things will always tug at its seams. The song of love is sung through respect and thoughtfulness for each other. They are the best assurance of a gracious and loving bond for years to come.

*B*y giving love, we become magnets of love.

The happiest people are those who give and receive love from their families and friends. Now, we're talking about the "no-strings-attached" kind of love.

*B*egin with the love you have. Love gratefully. This love expands your heart into a greater vessel which can hold yet more love.

*L*ove is all there is. It is the beginning and end of life.

FACING OURSELVES

*E*verything is a gift from God. The challenge is to understand what is happening to you.

*L*ife, through other people and situations, faces us with ourselves. It makes the weak stronger. The shy learn to be more outgoing. Helpless people are thrown upon their own resources, forcing them to help themselves.

*T*roubles come to us for our purification. They come because we must learn a divine law. Habits fall away once Soul (you) decides It wants spiritual realization more than Its vices.

$\mathcal{L}$earning means making errors. Those who are learning spiritually make errors just the way anyone does when he is growing.

*E*ach one of us is struggling with self-discipline. We find it in everything we do, in our job or at home. We have all these little things in our lives which are teaching us greater discipline.

A guiding rule that will stand you well throughout life is this saying: Is it true, is it necessary, is it kind?

Unless the answer is yes for all three, then you would do well to reconsider your intended action.

The spiritual student develops an inner link with the ECK, the Holy Spirit. Thus he taps into the Supreme Creative Force that guides him around all the blocks in his path that once defeated him.

*O*ne's ability to take charge of his own life increases. This is a solid step toward self-mastery and that state of consciousness called the kingdom of heaven.

*L*iving in the moment means integrating the lessons of yesterday into the actions of today.

$\mathcal{L}$ife is a stream of happy and un-happy experiences, because that leads to Soul's purification. How do you get by in the dark times? Try to give love to someone.

*B*e strong to the strong. Show kindness to the weak. Use resourcefulness to deal with people and situations that cause you problems. Life brings us face-to-face with ourselves.

CLIMBING THE SPIRITUAL LADDER

A spiritual path ought to show the way to God. If you find one that does this, then follow it. If not, you must find another that fits you.

$\mathscr{Y}$our goal can be anything, but it should be God-Realization—becoming one with Divine Spirit. Once we set that as our goal, then it depends on how fervently we want it.

*E*verything is within its rightful place in the Kingdoms of God.

An uncountable number of Souls exist in creation. There are also an endless number of forms in which Souls can find expression for spiritual unfoldment. The human form is but one of many.

We know that Soul exists by the evidence of life around us. When Soul inhabits a body, that body lives, moves, and has being. By direct and indirect evidence, we know that some unseen force gives life to a physical body.

What is that something? Soul.

*S*oul exists because God loves It.

God created Souls so that It (God) could come into an expanding awareness of Itself through their experiences of love and mercy toward others.

*T*his element of God—expanding awareness—also underlies the "plus element" of the ECK teachings. That is, there is always one more heaven. Always one more state of consciousness above the last.

*P*eople who *know*—actually know, not just believe—that Soul outlives death enjoy happy, creative lives.

The purpose of the Eckankar teachings is to give the individual proof of the nature of Soul in a way that is meaningful to him.

*T*he Mahanta, the Inner Master, is an expression of the Spirit of God that is always with you. You can ask in contemplation to see and know about the creation and nature of Soul. If you are sincere, the Mahanta will show you.

*T*he most important point of all is that you are Soul. Know that you are a spark of God and can exist fully only within the realization of that profound truth. As such, you are a light and inspiration to others.

ACCEPTING
CHANGE

---

*T*hings change. After all, isn't change the very nature of life? Nothing is ever the same.

$\mathcal{A}$ lesson learned early or late in the ECK teachings is that Soul can go in one of three ways in any stage of Its spiritual unfoldment. It can move forward, move backward, or stand still. That's it.

*B*eing born means having to learn
to care for ourselves in a society. Each of us
must learn how.

$\mathcal{G}$et experiences in work, in education, in your spiritual exercises, and in your personal relationships. The point is to live life with a loving, grateful heart.

*R*esponsibility is another face of love. At the crossroads of decision, ask the Mahanta, the Inner Master, what to do. He will tell you—by intuition, by knowing, or by direct speech—what decision is spiritually correct.

*E*ach life cycle has a growth and a
fulfillment stage. We switch back and forth
between them.

The growth phase moves on to the fulfillment stage. Here, we master the new routines that come with change and plunge into the options of our unexplored life. All our attention is upon the challenges and rewards before us.

*I*f something is valuable to you—a camera, a loved one, a state of mind—it pays not to neglect it.

The loss of a camera is a cheap lesson if it gets across the lesson of being careful with those things that have a special value for us.

Precious is as precious does.

$\mathcal{I}$t helps to know this world for what it is—good and evil. The love and guidance of the Mahanta, the Inner Master, helps you avoid many of the hard times and find the good.

The secret is this: You make your own happiness. And that begins with the company you keep.

*H*ere is a brief review of the final goal of Soul: It gathers an education in the lower worlds so that It can become a true citizen in the spiritual community. This is what we call a Co-worker with God.

PAST LIVES, DREAMS, AND SOUL TRAVEL

*N*o matter what we were in the past during any other life, we are spiritually greater today.

A Soul that completes a certain level of purification then graduates to a higher level of choice, experience, and service.

*H*istory can teach us much about how mankind's unlearned lessons repeat themselves. This allows us to use our knowledge to avoid unnecessary problems.

*W*e live the spiritual life beginning where we are today. We look to see the hand of Divine Spirit guiding us toward the greater consciousness, which leads us to becoming a more direct vehicle for Spirit.

A dream is a real experience. As Soul—the spiritual being you are as a divine spark of God—you can (and do) have hundreds of experiences going on side by side at different levels. So does everyone else.

*S*ome people naturally enjoy vivid recollections of their dream state, but those who don't can develop the skill.

*I*n Eckankar, dream study works on all levels. As with all things of a divine nature, accept each dream as a spiritual gift. Wonder about it. Roll it gently around in your mind to see whether loving patience will reveal its significance.

A good dream is one that helps you grow stronger, wiser, and more full of love.

A bad dream is generally a memory of a past life. Bad dreams are old fears.

So good and bad dreams both hold spiritual lessons.

*O*ur dreams prepare us for many future possibilities. We can then decide which future path we want to go for.

$\mathcal{S}$oul Travel is simply Soul's movement to God.

A dream is like something happening to us at arm's length.

Soul Travel is the real thing.

The reason Soul Travel is so full of
life is that in the Soul body we rise in consciousness. We are closer to the full awareness of ECK, Divine Spirit.

THE CHOICE IS YOURS

*P*eople who write off this world as temporal think it's a worthless place and so miss out on a lot of valuable unfoldment.

How do they think one reaches God-Realization? It's not by hiding from the world, but by swimming in life.

*F*ollow your heart. Learn the spiritual lessons in any given job. Then move on to a new challenge.

*I*f guided by divine love, we are more likely to change our minds when new information comes along.

Those under the guidance of the ECK, the Holy Spirit, are always alert.

If the Holy Spirit brings a new direction into your life, contemplate upon it. Be willing to change.

*T*he main purpose of the ECK teachings is to help people find their way back home to God, no matter what their circumstances in life.

*I*f the foods in your diet let you feel and act with love, charity, and wisdom, then diet makes no difference at all to your spirituality.

*M*ost times our body gets sick, it's trying to tell us something: to eat foods, wear clothes, or do some other thing that is better for us.

A healing depends a lot upon one's opening his heart to love.

The true healer is the ECK, Divine Spirit. When a healing takes place, it is through the power of the ECK.

$\mathcal{L}$ife is to cherish. Be respectful of all life, especially your own.

A heart person tends toward love, patience, and tolerance. He is like sunshine to others.

If you stay true to your mission in life, which is to become a Co-worker with God, the Holy Spirit and the Mahanta will guide you to the right places.

WHAT ARE THE SPIRITUAL EXERCISES OF ECK?

*T*he Spiritual Exercises of ECK are the golden key to a life of meaning and happiness.

*S*imple contemplations, in a way they
are equivalent to prayer.

*T*hrough this contemplative effort, we learn to listen to the Voice of God. The Voice of God is the Holy Spirit, which we call the ECK.

*I*f you practice the Spiritual Exercises of ECK on a regular schedule, like a meal, you'll get the inner nourishment you seek.

*E*xperiment with the spiritual exercises; try new things. You're in your own God Worlds. Ask yourself, am I learning something new every day from what I'm doing? Am I getting insight and help from within?

*A*nswers may not come during contemplation. Often they come later. But they do come.

*H*ow can we face life as we find it?
The key is always through the Spiritual Exercises of ECK.

*T*ry this simple spiritual exercise:

HU, this ancient name for God, is a love song to God. You can sing it. And in singing it or holding it in your mind during times of need, it becomes a prayer. It becomes a prayer of the highest sort.

*I*f you are successful with the spiritual exercises, you ought to become aware of either the Light or the Sound of God. You might meet the Inner Master, the Mahanta. He awaits the individual who is sincere in seeking truth.

Act as if. For example, if you want the Mahanta in your life as a spiritual guide, act as if he is.

*T*he spiritual exercises make you
(Soul) pure.

When you become pure enough in this
lifetime, you will never again have to return
to earth unless you want to help others find
spiritual freedom too. That's what the ECK
Masters do.

STEPS TO
SPIRITUAL
FREEDOM

We must first give to life if we expect anything in return. This is the divine law.

*T*he law of the universes is that one must pay in the true coin for everything received.

*E*arth is often a kettle of boiling water, but it's still the best place for Soul to find the purity of being.

*M*uch of the experience of people on the wheel of death and rebirth is *unconscious* experience. So they run in a circle. The Spiritual Exercises of ECK, however, lead to *conscious* experience. They go in the most direct way to God.

*P*ut all God qualities like patience and love together in yourself, and you will be a joy to all who know you.

*S*oul must use the earthly life to expand in consciousness via the Spiritual Exercises of ECK.

These exercises open a person's heart to God's love, which is to help and comfort all.

*E*very choice, as you're learning, bears a consequence.

*I*n a nutshell, your life today is the sum of all your past choices. So who's to blame for what? It all gets down to number one—us—as the creator of our own fortunes and misfortunes.

*S*o, every experience is a teacher. Keep up with your spiritual exercises. They open your heart to love divine.

A loving relationship is the first step to loving God. Love unties the bonds that anchor us to the material world of wants and desires. So divine love leads directly to spiritual freedom.

*T*he steps to spiritual freedom are these: (1) learn to love yourself, (2) learn to love others (human love), and (3) this will open your heart to love for God. That is the key to spiritual freedom.

Your journey to God begins at home.

How
ENLIGHTENMENT
COMES

*E*nlightenment is a gentle thing if it's right, if you're ready for it. It gives you a different viewpoint, a different state of consciousness.

*W*ith daily practice, you will find it easier and more natural to set goals through the art of visualization. You will then discover the secret for creating a happier, more successful life, because you will have a greater say over your dreams and desires.

We are a state of consciousness. Everyone and everything in our personal and universal world has an effect upon us. We want to become aware of what these effects are. Then we can sort through them, nurturing the good ones and discarding the bad.

*I*f we take responsibility and do something that gives us greater understanding, life becomes easier.

*S*ometimes there is something going on, something that's not too smooth for you. You can do a spiritual fast for a couple of days. You'll find that your attitude and your very words are different. You're not creating karma the way you were before.

*O*ne who communicates daily with the Word of God, the ECK, can only speak words of joy and reverence.

The Blue Star, or Blue Light, is one way the Mahanta often appears to someone at first. He is one with the ECK (Divine Spirit). So in the fullest sense the Blue Star, or Blue Light, is the ECK. You'll see it in contemplation.

The practice of the exercises forms a pact with the Inner Master. By doing them, an individual says, "Please help me work out my karma and find God."

The white light is the Light of God. HU is the Sound of God. The Light and Sound are the two most trusted pillars of protection that one can ever find.

As you progress in the Light and Sound of God, the ECK (Divine Spirit) will begin to enliven your spiritual pulse. You will begin to listen, and you will hear the Sound of the spheres, which may sound like the wind in the trees.

*F*ill yourself with love. Then you will learn everything you ever need to know about God and life.

WORKING WITH THE SPIRITUAL LAWS OF LIFE

All real success is about love. Success is hard to come by, but love can make it happen.

*H*ow can you forgive yourself? Just do it. Apologize, then, for your thoughtless behavior and try to do better next time.

A higher law is the Law of Love. With this law comes the understanding that indeed what will be will be. But the difference here is that we do not wish or expect others to get punished for their misdeeds. Instead, we give them love in return.

The Law of Karma, yet another facet of the Law of Love, purifies people by holding them responsible for their thoughts and deeds, both to themselves and others.

*T*hen what is karma for? It is to spiritually uplift each Soul.

A Soul may intentionally choose a hard life to learn more about love, wisdom, and charity. Pain, like joy, is simply a tool in the toolbox of karma and rebirth.

To grow spiritually, we move beyond a strict acceptance of karma and thus take the high road to God.

*Y*ou answer to a higher law: divine love. Use your spiritual powers of creation for the good of all.

*T*he Law of Silence is a spiritual principle that draws a very fine line. If you have an experience that may help another person understand his own, then tell it in a fitting way. You can tell when you've said too much.

*I*n order to know when to speak and when to remain silent, you must first apply the Law of Discrimination.

*B*e sure of the people you would entrust with the dreams of your heart. Heed the old saying: Never lend more than you can stand to lose.

The ECK provides you with life. But there are rules, spiritual laws, that are a part of living. Now here's where the play of free will comes in. You have the choice of following or breaking the rules—all, some, or none of them.

So learn and obey the spiritual laws early. Life is more pleasant then.

THE SECRET
OF SERVING
ALL LIFE

Service must first begin by loving yourself and loving your family as you love God. Unless you can love yourself first, you cannot love your neighbor.

*F*acing life gracefully is the first step to giving of yourself to others.

*B*eing graceful in your dealings with other people and in giving of yourself to life go together. They complement each other.

*L*ife has ways to insure that people learn humility. Because how can you truly serve anyone—whether it's yourself, your family, your neighbor, or God—unless there is humility?

The key to bringing divine love to us is to first give selflessly of ourselves in some way, without any thought of reward.

*W*e're all creations of God, and for this reason, each Soul deserves the highest respect you can give.

*L*oneliness is Soul's desire to find God. The Spiritual Exercises of ECK bring the Light and Sound of God.

*S*ervice to God is a natural outcome for all who do the Spiritual Exercises of ECK every day. They learn to travel in the other worlds. There they find the spiritual benefits of ECK, which are companionship, life, hope, love, peace, and self-reliance.

*D*ivine love enters the heart in a direct line from the Light and Sound of God. Those who become open channels for these twin blessings of ECK shine with the certainty of life.

Service to others is a natural out-pouring of one's love for life.

*W*hat is the secret of service? In a word, love.

THE LOVING HEART

*M*any people do not understand that life, with its burdens, is a treasure. The weight of disappointment makes us close our eyes to the gift of being in the world to learn about the loving heart.

*L*et love be what it will. Just love without expecting its return.

*D*ivine love is joyful, thankful. It gives itself fully.

*S*oul is here to learn how to become more like God's pure qualities of love. We learn most from our troubles, not always from the good times.

*D*o everything, large or small, as if you were doing it for God alone. That means the task will be done with love, joy, and (don't forget) thoroughness.

There is a spiritual side to every experience or event, no matter how large or small, and whether or not it occurs in everyday life or in a dream.

*O*n earth, the common state of awareness is the human consciousness. As one learns more about love and humility through the trials of many lifetimes, he moves higher in consciousness.

*O*ften we want enlightenment because the life we have today is hard. But the true reason for spiritual enlightenment is not to escape this life but to learn how to live it richly, to enjoy it.

*O*nly those with a loving heart ever get to drink of the living water of life. Many may find it, but only those who come with love in their hearts will know what to give to drink of it, to receive truth.

$\mathcal{G}$od-Realization is a state of wonder and bliss beyond words. It's Soul's destiny.

In time, divine love will take you to the top of the spiritual mountain. There, you will experience the wonders of Self- and God-Realization in the proper seasons of your life.

And, in the end, you will love God completely.

ABOUT THE AUTHOR

Author Harold Klemp is known as a pioneer of today's focus on "everyday spirituality." He was raised on a Wisconsin farm and attended divinity school. He also served in the U.S. Air Force.

In 1981, after years of training, he became the spiritual leader of Eckankar, Religion of the Light and Sound of God. His mission is to help people find their way back to God in this life.

Harold Klemp speaks each year to thousands of seekers at Eckankar seminars. Author of more than seventy-five books, he continues to write, including many articles and spiritual-study discourses. Harold Klemp's inspiring and practical approach to spirituality helps thousands of people worldwide find greater freedom, wisdom, and love in their lives.

ALSO BY
HAROLD KLEMP

Available at bookstores, online booksellers,
or directly from:
Eckankar
PO Box 2000, Chanhassen, MN 55317-2000 USA.
Tel (952) 380-2222 Fax (952) 380-2196
www.Eckankar.org

Immortality of Soul Series
The Language of Soul
Love—The Keystone of Life
Truth Has No Secrets
Touching the Face of God
The Awakened Heart
HU, the Most Beautiful Prayer

A selected list:
The Call of Soul
The Spiritual Exercises of ECK
The Spiritual Laws of Life
Past Lives, Dreams, and Soul Travel